The Dalai Lama's
Historic Visit to North America

Teachings of
His Holiness The Dalai Lama

Edited and Photographed by Marcia Keegan

Clear Light Publications Inc.

Preface . . . . *Tenzin N. Tethong*
Acting Representative of His Holiness

Introduction and Editorial Consultant . . . . *Tinley Nyandak*
of the Office of Tibet

Editorial Consultant . . . . *Valerie M. Shepherd*

Design Consultant . . . . *Bo Zaunders*

Production Manager . . . . *Alise Creque*

Logo Design . . . . *Thupten Norbu*

I would like to thank, first, His Holiness the Dalai Lama for his wisdom and for sharing with us the blessing of his presence and his teachings in North America, and I would also like to thank my friends who helped me in the preparation of this book: Celesta Birnbaum, Tenzin Choegel, Alise Creque, Harmon Houghton, Sally Lloyd, Thupten Norbu, Tinley Nyandak, Thupten Phelgye, Rev. Ellen Resch, Sherpa Rimpoche, Valerie Shepherd. Tenzin Tethong, Barbara Weisberg, and Bo Zaunders.

© Copyright Clear Light Publications, Inc., 1981.
P.O. Box 2520
New York, New York 10163

ISBN 0-940666-00-6

Library of Congress Catalog Number 81-68-209.

Preface

It is my distinct pleasure to introduce this excellent book of His Holiness the Dalai Lama's visit to North America: a historic first visit ever by a Dalai Lama to the United States and Canada in 1979 and 1980.

During these visits, His Holiness travelled extensively across Canada and the United States and spoke to a cross section of people from all walks of life. Beyond the symbolic importance of this visit, His Holiness communicated his ideas of peace and compassion most profoundly.

Newly settled Tibetan immigrants, and Mongolians who had left their homelands many generations ago once again renewed their ancient ties with the Dalai Lama; and thousands of others found renewed commitment and hope in His Holiness' message of humanity and love.

His Holiness often said that he was most touched by the warmth of reception everywhere, and felt encouraged to see so many who showed the same concerns for the problems facing human society today.

This book not only recalls the excitement and enthusiasm that prevailed during the visits, but in its own way furthers His Holiness' universal message of shared concern and compassion.

Tenzin N. Tethong
Acting Representative of
His Holiness the Dalai Lama

Introduction

His Holiness the 14th Dalai Lama, Tenzin Gyatso, is the spiritual and temporal leader of the Tibetan people. He was born on July 6, 1935, in a small village called Taktser, in north eastern Tibet. Born to a peasant family, His Holiness was recognized at the age of two, in accordance with Tibetan tradition, as the reincarnation of His predecessor the 13th Dalai Lama.

In His autobiography, His Holiness writes: "I have always felt that if I had been born in a rich or aristocratic family, I would not have been able to appreciate the feelings and sentiments of the humble classes of Tibetans. But, owing to my lowly birth, I can understand them and read their minds, and that is why I feel for them so strongly and have tried my best to improve their lot in life."

The Dalai Lamas are the manifestations of the Buddha of Compassion who chose to take rebirth for the purpose of serving other human beings. Dalai Lama means Ocean of Wisdom. Tibetans normally refer to His Holiness as Yeshe Norbu, *the Wish-fulfilling Gem or simply* Kundun, *meaning The Presence.*

When the 13th Dalai Lama had passed away in 1933, the task which confronted the Tibetan Government was not to simply appoint a successor but to seek for and discover a child in whom the Buddha of Compassion would incarnate. It was not necessary that the child should have been born just at the time of the death of His predecessor, or even very soon after it.

As on former occasions, there would be indications of the directions in which the search should be made, and that the child would be found to possess physical and mental attributes similar to those of His predecessor. For instance, when the 13th Dalai Lama's body was laid in the shrine, facing south, it was found twice that His head turned to the east. And to the east of the new shrine, on a pillar of well-seasoned wood set in a great block of stone, on the east side of the pillar, there appeared a great fungus. Many other signs also indicated that the next Dalai Lama should be sought in the east.

In 1935, the Regent of Tibet went to the sacred lake of Lhamoe Lhatso at Chokhorgyal about 90 miles southeast of Lhasa, Tibet's capital. The Tibetans have observed that visions of the future can be seen in this lake. The regent saw the vision of three Tibetan letters: "Ah," "Ka" and "Ma," followed by a picture of a monastery with roofs of jade green and gold and a house with turquoise tiles. A detailed description of these visions were written down and kept a strict secret.

In 1937, high lamas and dignitaries, carrying the secrets of the visions, were sent to all parts of Tibet to search for the place which the regent had seen in the waters. The search party which headed east was under the leadership of Lama Kewtsang Rinpoche of Sera Monastery. When they arrived in Amdo, they found a place matching the description of the secret vision. The party went to the house with Kewtsang Rinpoche disguised as a servant and junior official Lobsang Tsewang disguised as the leader. The Rinpoche was wearing a rosary which belonged to the 13th Dalai Lama, and the little boy recognizing it, demanded that it should be given to him. Kewtsang Rinpoche promised to give it to him if he could guess who he was, and the boy replied that he was Sera aga, which meant in the local dialect, "a Lama of Sera." Then Rinpoche asked who the leader was and the boy gave his name correctly. He also knew the name of the real servant. This was followed by a series of tests which included choosing of correct articles which belonged to the 13th Dalai Lama.

By these tests, they were further convinced that the reincarnation had been found and their conviction was enhanced by the vision of three letters: "Ah" stood for Amdo, name of the province; "Ka" stood for Kumbum, one of the largest monasteries in the neighborhood; or the two letters "Ka" and "Ma" stood for the monastery of Karma Rolpai Dorjee on the mountain above the village. It was also significant that once the 13th Dalai Lama had stayed at the monastery on His way back from China. In 1940, the new Dalai Lama was enthroned.

He began His education at the age of six and completed the Geshe Lharampa Degree (Doctorate of Buddhist Philosophy) when He was 25. At 24, His Holiness took the preliminary examinations at each of the three monastic universities: Drepung, Sera and Ganden. The final examination was held in the Jokhang, Lhasa, during the annual Monlam Festival of prayer which is held in the first month of each year.

In the morning He was examined on logic by 30 scholars turn by turn in congregational discussion. In the afternoon, 15 scholars took part as His opponents in the debate on the Middle Path, and in the evening 35 scholars tested His knowledge of the canon of monastic discipline and the study of metaphysics. His Holiness passed the examination with honors.

In 1950, when He was only 16, He was called upon to assume full political power when Tibet was threatened by the might of China. In 1954, His Holiness went to Peking to talk peace with Mao Tse-tung and other Chinese leaders including Chou En-lai and Deng Xiaoping. In 1956, His Holiness visited India to attend the 2500th Buddha Jayanti Anniversary. While in India, His Holiness had a series of meetings with Prime Minister Nehru and Premier Chou En-lai about deteriorating conditions in Tibet. In 1959, His Holiness was forced into exile in India after the Chinese military occupation of Tibet. Since that time, His Holiness has been residing in Dharamsala, the seat of the Tibetan Government-in-exile. Dharamsala is aptly known as "Little Lhasa" where there are also many Tibetan educational and cultural institutions such as the Tibetan Medical School, the Institute of Tibetan Performing Arts, Namgyal Monastery and so forth.

While in exile, His Holiness appealed to the United Nations on the question of Tibet, resulting in three resolutions adopted by the General Assembly in 1959, 1961 and 1965. His Holiness has set up educational, cultural and religious institutions which have contributed significantly towards the preservation of the Tibetan identity and its rich heritage. In 1963, His Holiness promulgated a draft constitution of Tibet which assures a democratic form of government. Unlike His predecessors, His Holiness has traveled to North America, Western Europe, the United Kingdom, Japan, Thailand and met with religious leaders of these countries.

During His travels abroad, His Holiness has spoken strongly for better understanding and respect among the different faiths of the world. Towards this end, His Holiness has made numerous appearances in interfaith services, imparting the message of universal responsibility, love, compassion and kindness. "The need for simple human to human relationship is becoming increasingly urgent. . . . Today the world is smaller and more interdependent. One nation's problems can no longer be solved by itself completely. Thus, without a sense of universal responsibility, our very survival becomes threatened. Basically, universal responsibility is feeling for other people's suffering just as we feel our own. It is the realization that even our enemy is entirely motivated by the quest for happiness. We must recognize that all beings want the same thing that we want. This is the way to achieve a true understanding, unfettered by artificial consideration."

Tinley Nyandak
The Office of Tibet

Photographer's Note

In the fall of 1979, I travelled in the United States with the Dalai Lama, and then in the fall of 1980 I again travelled with His Holiness on his tours throughout Canada.

The photos presented here, together with selected excerpts from his teachings in the United States and Canada, represent some of the highlights of both trips. Since this book is not designed as an exact record, the text that accompanies the pictures is not necessarily excerpted from speeches delivered at the location portrayed. All text in the first, or United States portion, of the book, however, is excerpted from talks given in the United States, and the same holds true for the Canadian portion of the book. Some of these teachings were given in English, in His Holiness' own words, and some were given in Tibetan, simultaneously translated into English by Professor Jeffrey Hopkins.

Between these two trips I travelled to the Himalayas, where I offered Buddhist monasteries copies of the picture I had taken in California which is now on the cover of this book. For the Buddhist monks I met, even a photograph of the Dalai Lama symbolized so much, that they immediately put it on their altars. The following month, my friend Thupten Phelgye, a Tibetan monk from Nechung Monastery in Dharamsala, India, was travelling in Ladakh. When he saw the pictures of His Holiness in the monasteries, he knew that I had been there.

I initially had decided to follow the tours of the Dalai Lama in the United States and Canada out of personal interest; I stayed because it had become one of the most important experiences of my life.

I'm honored to help in sharing these teachings that His Holiness gave on his first historic visit to the Western Hemisphere.

Marcia Keegan

My message is the practice of compassion, love and kindness.

These things are very useful in our daily life, and also for the whole of human society these practices can be very important.

The scene is a small crowded room at the Freedom House in New York City. It is the Dalai Lama's first press conference in the United States. A voice somewhere in the back of the room asks, "Your Holiness, do you have a message for the United States?"

"Compassion," replies His Holiness the Dalai Lama XIV, emanating a happy and peaceful radiance.

Asked about the purpose of His Holiness' visit to the United States, he answered, "My visit has no particular purpose. I am a citizen of this world. As a Buddhist monk, in my mind all people are the same. I always have great respect for different systems. I have learned tolerance and compassion and kindness. I always want to go to as many places as I can and learn many things."

Every segment of the Buddhist Community wanted to honor the Dalai Lama. One Fall morning 1,000 people gathered outdoors at a Tibetan Buddhist monastery in Washington, New Jersey to hear His Holiness speak from an altar surrounded by tankas. The scents of blooming flowers and incense mingled sweetly in the sunlight, and the scene looked like Lhasa must have in the old days. There were around 200 Buddhists in ceremonial robes present, and Geshe Wangyal, the 79-year-old Director of the monastery, who had known His Holiness as a child, was beaming.

The kindness and happiness in the Dalai Lama's smiling face revealed the perfected practice of what he was teaching. While he spoke, a white butterfly circled his head; his students spoke reverently of the solitary pink rose that had bloomed during the night outside the monastery where he was staying.

The Venerable Geshe Wangyal founded the Lamaist Buddhist Monastery of America in the Kalmuck-Mongolian community of Freewood Acres, New Jersey, in 1958. As the first Tibetan Buddhist monastery in the United States, it supported many Kalmucks in maintaining their traditional Buddhist worship and laid the groundwork for the spread of Buddhist teachings to Americans.

Geshe Wangyal is a lama from the Drepung Monastery in Tibet where he received the geshe degree, comparable to a Western doctorate. Geshe Wangyal also studied extensively in China and Mongolia before arriving in the United States in 1955.

Wherever I go, I always give the advice to be altruistic and kind to others. And from my own point of view, I am now 44 years old, and I am concentrating my own energies, meditation and so forth, on the increase of kindness. This is essential, essential Buddhadharma.

Great compassion is the root of all forms of worship.

Whether one believes in a religion or not, and whether one believes in rebirth or not, there isn't anyone who doesn't appreciate compassion, mercy.

Right from the moment of our birth, we are under the care and kindness of our parents. And then later on in our life when we are oppressed by sickness and become old, we are again dependent on the kindness of others. And since at the beginning and end of our lives, we are so dependent on others' kindness, how can it be in the middle that we would neglect kindness towards others?

If one assumes a humble attitude, one's own good qualities will increase. Whereas if one is proud, one will become jealous of others, one will become angry with others, and one will look down on others, and due to that, there will be unhappiness in society.

One of the basic points is kindness. With kindness, with love and compassion, with this feeling that is the essence of brotherhood, sisterhood, one will have inner peace. This compassionate feeling is the basis of inner peace.

With anger, hatred, it is very difficult to feel inner peace. It is on this point that various different religious faiths all have the same emphasis. In every major world religion, the emphasis is on brotherhood.

His Holiness the Dalai Lama speaking at the Lamaist Buddhist Monastery in Washington, New Jersey. ▶

Under the bright sun, in this beautiful park, many of us are gathered here with different languages, different styles of dress, perhaps even different faiths. However, all of us are the same in being humans, and we all uniquely have the thought of "I," and we're all the same in wanting happiness and in wanting to avoid suffering.

But at the root, there are two kinds of pleasure and suffering. There are physical and mental pleasure and physical and mental suffering. Our materalistic progress is for the sake of achieving that happiness which depends on the body, and in getting rid of that suffering which depends on the body. However, it is indeed difficult, isn't it, for us to get rid of all suffering by these external means. And thus there comes to be a great difference between seeking happiness by dependence on material things, and in seeking happiness in dependence on one's own internal thought. Although the basic suffering is the same, there comes to be a great difference in the way we experience this, dependent on our attitude. Therefore, mental attitude is very important with respect to how we spend our lives.

A good mind, a good heart, warm feelings—these are the most important things. If you don't have such a good mind, you yourself cannot function. One cannot be happy, and so also one's own kin, one's own mate or children or neighbors and so forth won't be happy either.

And thus from nation to nation and continent to continent everyone's mind becomes disturbed, people lose happiness. But then, on the other hand, if one does have a good attitude, a good mind, a good heart, then the opposite is true.

Thus in human society, love, compassion and kindness are the most important. It is something really precious; it is very necessary in one's life. So it is worthwhile to make effort to develop this sort of good, good heart.

There is no need to mention the great difference between the amount of satisfaction there is in just one's self being happy and the amount of satisfaction there is in an infinite number of people being happy.

If even one person cannot stand suffering, what need is there to mention how all people can't stand suffering? Therefore it is a mistake if one uses others for one's own purpose; rather one should use oneself for others' welfare. Thus one should use whatever capacities of body, speech and mind one has for the benefit of others: That is right. Thus it is necessary to generate such a mind of altruism wishing for the welfare of others, through their achievement of happiness and through their getting rid of suffering.

Two altars at the Lamaist Buddhist Monastery in Washington, New Jersey; the one on the left displays Maitreya, the coming Buddha, with a portrait of His Holiness the Dalai Lama.

It is in dependence upon sentient beings that one first generates this altruistic aspiration to highest enlightenment, and it is in relation to sentient beings that one practices the deeds of the path in order to achieve enlightenment, and it is for the sake of sentient beings that one achieves Buddhahood. Therefore, sentient beings are the object of observation, the basis of all of this marvellous development, therefore they are more important than even the wish-granting jewel, and one should treat them respectfully and kindly.

A Mongolian-American boy being helped by elder monks to prepare for His Holiness' visit to the Buddhist Monastery at Washington, New Jersey. The boy is now in India studying Buddhism.

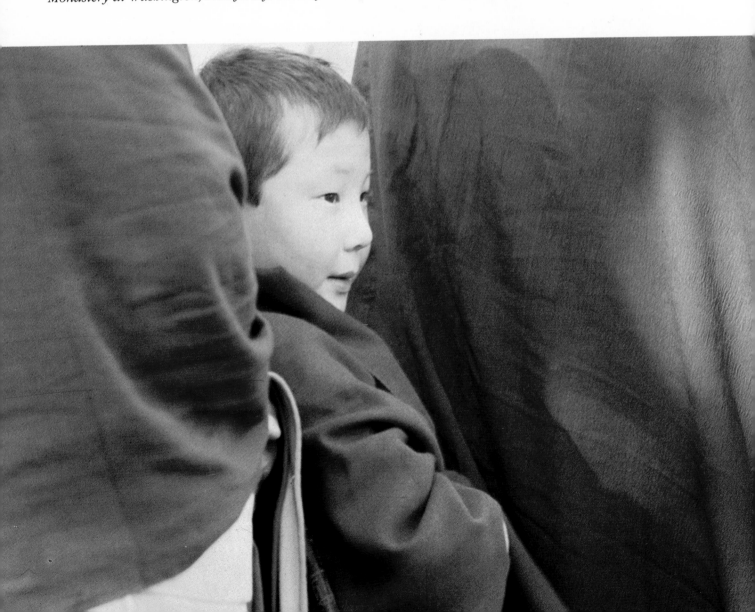

Geshe Thupten Wangyal holding an offering of incense to welcome His Holiness to the Lamaist Buddhist Monastery at Washington, New Jersey.

With regard to the Bodhisattva vehicle, there is no practice that is not included within the basic motivation of consciously seeking the highest enlightenment of the Buddha for the sake of all living beings, this being induced by love and compassion and attained through the practice of the Six Perfections.

Inner darkness, which we call ignorance, is the root of suffering. The more inner light that comes, the more darkness will diminish. This is the only way to achieve salvation or Nirvana.

Mandala offerings of ingredients of different stones symbolizing the offering of the universe to the Triple Gem, which is composed of the Buddha, the Dharma, and the religious community.

The principles that are set forth in the Theravada scriptures revolve around wisdom, selflessness, and the practice of meditation which includes the development of the 37 harmonies with enlightenment. These truths have as their basis the good effort of not harming others. Therefore, their basis is compassion.

Thupten Phelgye, from Nechung Monastery in Dharamsala, India, holding a butter sculpture.

Calm abiding of the mind, meditative stabilization, and wisdom are the weapons. Wisdom is like the bullet or the ammunition, and the calm mind is like the weapon for firing.

Just as when we fight external suffering, we have to undergo suffering, and so forth, so when we undergo the strife internally, there is indeed internal pain. Therefore, religion is something internal to be thought about.

Seven water bowls on the altar at the Buddhist Monastery in Washington, New Jersey. The seven water bowls represent seven steps taken by the Lord Buddha at the time of his birth.

His Holiness giving a sermon at the Buddhist Monastery in Washington, New Jersey.

One's own anger, pride and so forth serve as obstacles to the development of one's own altruistic attitude. They harm it. They injure it. Therefore, one shouldn't just let these go on when they are generated, but, by relying on antidotes, stop them.

Anger, pride, competitiveness and so forth are our real enemies. So, since there isn't anybody who hasn't gotten angry at some time, we can on the basis of our own experience understand that no one can be happy with an attitude of anger.

What doctor is there who prescribes anger as a treatment for any disease? What doctor is there who says that by getting angry you can make yourself more happy?

Now I am going to tell something about how to develop this compassion.

First of all, it is important to understand that between self and others, others are far more important, because others are far more numerous.

If you don't use the imagination just to make up something, sometimes the imagination can be used very effectively in order to understand a point. Therefore, in your mind please imagine that on one side is one party, made up of all beings, an infinite number of beings. And on the other side, imagine another party, that is to say, your single, selfish self.

Now you're thinking as a third person. Now, if you think properly, would you go to this side with this single, selfish man, or to this side, with the limitless other? Naturally, you will feel much closer to the limitless other, because of the number of beings.

But both are the same human beings. Both have a desire for happiness. The only difference is number. So, if limitless number is much more important, then naturally you will join this party.

In this way, you can see that others are far more important than oneself and that all of one's own capacity could be used for the benefit of others.

Anger, hatred, jealousy—it is not possible to find peace with them. Through compassion, through love, we can solve many problems; we can have true happiness, real disarmament.

One of the most important things is compassion. We cannot buy it in one of New York City's big shops. You cannot produce it by machine. But by inner development, yes. Without inner peace, it is impossible to have world peace.

Tibetan monks blowing gyalings at St. Patrick's Cathedral, in New York City.

His Holiness the Dalai Lama and His Eminence Terence Cardinal Cooke, Archbishop of New York, at St. Patrick's Cathedral in New York City.

The Christians and Buddhists have basically the same teaching, the same aim. The world now becomes smaller and smaller and smaller, due to good communications and other factors also. With that development, different faiths and different cultures also come closer and closer. This is, I think, very good. If you understand each other's way of living, thinking, different philosophies and different faiths, it can help toward mutual understanding. To understand each other, naturally, we will develop respect for each other. From that, we develop true harmony and the ability to make joint efforts. And I always feel that this special inner development is something very important for mankind.

The Dalai Lama greeting a crowd of over 6,000 people at St. Patrick's Cathedral in New York City, after being introduced by Cardinal Cooke.

The Dalai Lama meeting with members of the Senate Foreign Relations Committee. After the meeting, Senator Jacob K. Javits, Republican of New York, said, ''His Holiness is a fabulous man, a devoted patriot and he gave us the impression that he was the symbol of Freedom.''

His Holiness at Capitol Hill, in Washington, D.C.

Congressman Charles Rose of North Carolina presents His Holiness with the traditional Tibetan white scarf (khata) at a reception in Washington, D.C.

The significance of His Holiness' visit to the United States was summed up for all Americans by Representative Charles Rose. Introducing the Dalai Lama before a public lecture His Holiness gave at Constitution Hall in Washington, Representative Rose said, "This is a holy instant for all Americans....Enlightenment starts with individuals. And if America is to cope with its current level of dilemmas, it must reach a higher level of consciousness than the level on which our problems were created. And the belief of Tibetan Buddhism in the evolution of the individual is harmonious with the desire of a growing number of our citizens for spiritual growth to reach a higher consciousness....Let us seek the path of love and higher consciousness and personal transformation. His Holiness is a guide to Enlightenment."

His Holiness addressing an audience at the Constitution Hall, in Washington, D.C.

In Los Angeles, His Holiness met with Elders of the Hopi Indians, who drove all night from Arizona, and he met with Chiefs from the Iroquois Confederacy in Syracuse. The meeting between the Tibetan and Native American spiritual leaders signified the culmination of ancient prophecies going back thousands of years.

According to a ninth century Tibetan prophecy, "When the iron bird flies, the Dharma (Buddhist teachings) will go west to the land of the Red Man."

According to a Hopi Indian prophecy, Pahana, a true spiritual being whose name is derived from salt water, would come from the East. He is the Sun Clan brother, whose return would mark the completion of a millenium-long ritual. The name Dalai Lama means "Teacher who is an Ocean of Wisdom."

Some mysterious relationship between the Hopi and Tibetan peoples seems to be reflected in their languages. In Hopi language, the word "nyima" means moon. In Tibetan, the same word means sun. The word "dawa" means moon in Tibetan, sun in Hopi.

Hopi means "peace," and these people regard themselves as the first inhabitants of North America. Their village at Old Oraibi is the oldest continuously occupied settlement in the United States. The Hopi leaders knew of the Tibetan prophecy, which foretold the spread of Buddhist teachings in the land of the Indian. Bearing in mind that their own prophecy told of a spiritual being who would come to them from the east, they were determined to explain the Hopi prophecy to the Dalai Lama.

Both Indians and Tibetans share a reverence for the earth and its creatures which greatly predates the contemporary concern for ecology.

No one knows what will happen in a few decades or a few centuries, what adverse effect, for example, deforestation might have on the weather, the soil, the rain.

We are having problems because people are concentrating on their selfish interests, on making money, and not thinking of the community as a whole. They are not thinking of the earth and the long term effects on man as a whole. If we of the present generation do not think about them now, the future generation might not be able to cope with them.

His Holiness greeting Hopi Elders. (Left to right): Earl Pela, Thomas Banyacya and David Monongye, in Los Angeles, California.

Love is an active human condition. When certain problems arise, you will feel hate, you may feel anger. In order to practice tolerance, first you have to control anger. Some people might think that it is better to express your anger than to control it. But within our conceptions, there are two types, one which it is better to control and one which is better not to control. One type of conceptions is thoughts which lead to depression and so forth. With those, it is definitely helpful if you are able to express those thoughts. However, there is a whole different class of conceptions such as hatred and love, which, when they are expressed once, aren't used up, they just increase. We can, in our own experience, understand that when desire and hatred and so forth are generated, we can watch them and figure out techniques by which we can lessen them. Through my own little experience, I can show you. If we can control some of our anger, which we can change ourselves, and if, on the other hand, we can think of the importance of other people's welfare, and practice in this way, then it is possible to achieve these good attitudes.

You see, practice of this is ultimately of benefit to ourselves. If you are truly selfish, wisely selfish, this practice gives you real calmness, and with inner calmness and peace you can handle all these problems with ease.

In our human life, tolerance is very important. If you have tolerance, you can easily overcome difficulties. If you have either little tolerance or are without it, then the smallest thing immediately irritates you. In a difficulty, you may overreact. In my own experience, I've had many questions, many feelings, and one of these feelings is that tolerance is something world-wide to practice in our human society.

So who teaches you tolerance? Maybe sometimes your children teach you patience, but always your enemy will teach you tolerance. So your enemy is really your teacher. If you have respect for your enemy, instead of anger, your compassion will develop. That type of compassion is real compassion which is based upon sound beliefs.

Usually you allow kindness toward family members. This kindness is inspired by affection, desire. Because of that, when the object of your compassion changes in aspect, becomes a little rough, then your own feeling changes also. That kind of compassion or love is not right. Therefore, it is necessary in the beginning to train these good attitudes.

When it says that one should be patient and withstand trouble, it doesn't mean that one should be defeated, should be overcome. The very purpose of engaging in the practice of patience is to become stronger in mind, stronger in heart. And also you want to remain calm. In that atmosphere of calmness, you can use real human beings to learn wisdom. If you lose patience, if your brain founders by emotions, then you've lost the power to analyze. But if you are patient, from a basis of altruism, then you don't lose your strength of mind; you can even increase your strength of mind and then use your powers of analysis to figure out ways to overcome the negative force that is opposing you. That's another question.

Material facilities, material encounters are very necessary for a human society, a country, a nation. It is absolutely necessary. At the same time, material progress and prosperity in itself could not produce inner peace; inner peace should come from within. So, that much depends upon our own attitude toward life, toward others, particularly toward problems. When two persons are facing the same kind of problem, because of different mental attitudes, for one person it is much easier to face the problem. So you see, it's the internal viewpoint that makes the difference.

When one gives one's kindness for the sake of getting something back in return, for the sake of getting a good name, for the sake of causing other people to like oneself, if the motive is for self, then this would not be really be a Bodhisattva deed. Therefore, one-pointedness points to giving only for helping others.

From all points of view we're all the same in wanting happiness and not wanting suffering. Now oneself is only one, but others are infinite in number. Therefore, others are more important than oneself.

Whether one believes in a religion or not, and whether one believes in rebirth or not, there isn't anyone who doesn't appreciate compassion, mercy.

His Holiness the Dalai Lama at Claremont College, California.

His Holiness speaking from the dais at Claremont College, California.

*In California, the Dalai Lama was invited to give a public lecture by the
Asian Studies Society of the University of California. The lecture stage
was a panoply of multi-colored robes. On one side sat Buddhist monks
of various nationalities dressed in maroon and yellow; on the other side
the western scholars sat dressed in their flowing black doctoral robes.
His Holiness was presented with an honorary degree in Asian Studies.*

Compassion and love are precious things in life. It is not complicated. It is simple, but difficult to practice.

Compassion can be put into practice if one recognizes the fact that every human being is a member of humanity and the human family regardless of differences in religion, culture, color and creed. Deep down, there is no difference.

His Holiness the Dalai Lama at age four: A photograph displayed at the Newark Museum in Newark, New Jersey.

If we put to use our more subtle consciousnesses, there will be that many more things that we can use the mind for. Therefore, qualities that begin in the mind can be increased limitlessly.

There should be a balance between material and spiritual progress, through the principles based on love and compassion. Love and compassion are the essence of all religion.

All religions can learn from each other; the ultimate goal of all religion is to produce better human beings. Better human beings would be more tolerant, more compassionate and less selfish.

The Dalai Lama at the Newark Museum, in New Jersey.

I believe that because of Tibetan art and culture, many foreign visitors come to Tibetan settlements in India to meet Tibetans. At the beginning we ourselves did not notice certain things, certain thinking, but these foreigners, after visiting, expressed, "Why you Tibetans have some sort of honest, happy life—very good despite your suffering. What is your secret?"

There is no secret. But I thought to myself, our culture is very much based on compassion. We are used to saying all the time, always, "All sentient beings are our fathers and mothers." Even someone who looks like a ruffian or a robber is still someone who has on his mind, "All mothers, all sentient beings." So I myself always practice this thinking. I think that is the real cause of happiness.

We are going into deep outer space, based on developments of modern technology. However, there are many things left to be examined and thought about with respect to the nature of the mind, what the substantial core of the mind is, what the corroborative condition of the mind is and so forth. There is much advice, many precepts with respect to this, but the meaning of all of these is love and compassion. Within the Buddhist doctrine, there are very many powerful techniques capable of advancing the mind with respect to compassion and love.

His Holiness the Dalai Lama at an altar in the Tibetan Collection of the Newark Museum in New Jersey.

Some of you might feel that you lose your independence if you don't let your mind just wander where it wants to, if you try to control it. But that is not the case.

If your mind is proceeding in the correct way, one already has the correct opinion. But if your mind is proceeding in an incorrect way, then it's necessary, definitely, to exercise control.

If you ask, "Is it possible to completely get rid of afflicted emotions, or is it necessary to just suppress them on the spot," then the answer is that from the Buddhist point of view, the conventional nature of mind is that it is a clear light. And from the ultimate point of view, it is also a clear light. So from the conventional point of view, these afflicted emotions are only extraneous and can be removed totally.

It is said that someone who acts as an enemy towards oneself is one's best teacher. Now, in dependence on teachers, one can learn about the importance of being patient, but can't get any opportunity actually to be patient. However, the actual practice of implementing patience comes when meeting with an enemy.

If we understand the oneness of human kind, then we realize the differences are secondary. With an attitude of respect and concern for other people, we can experience an atmosphere of happiness. That way we can create real harmony, real brotherhood. Through your own experience, try to be patient. You can change your attitude. If you practice continuously, you can change. The human mind has such potential— learn to train it.

The questions and answers presented below were compiled from the Dalai Lama's numerous public and private lectures, scholarly seminars, private meetings, and news conferences throughout his visit. They represent the broad spectrum of issues addressed when the spiritual leader of Tibetan Buddhism visited the United States.

Q: How do you feel Tibetan Buddhism is being practiced in America?

A: *The important thing is to get the essence. In Tibetan Buddhism there are a great variety of practices and many different methods of practicing. All are beneficial. At the same time, while taking the essence, there might be certain traditional ways of practicing which might have to undergo change in order to adjust the new environment or social structure. In the past, when a religion has gone from its native country to a new land, the essence was brought. Then, within that new land, it developed and adjusted to new circumstances. Something similar should happen to Tibetan Buddhism. So, it is your responsibility. I don't know.*

Q: Do you think the West can learn from Tibetans?

A: *I think so.*

Q: You were trained as a monk from childhood. Should American children be trained in a system from an early age, or should we wait until later?

A: *There are two ways to enter into Buddhism; one through faith and one through reasoning. At present, in this century, on this earth, in this period—for a Buddhist, faith alone may not be sufficient. So, reasoning is very important. Because of this, it would be better for someone to be trained later. But nevertheless, it would make a difference if a child knows the influence within the family from a very young age.*

Q: Do you think that the Tibetan Buddhism practiced in America is authentic?

A: *It depends to a great extent on the people who are teaching it, who are giving the teaching.*

Q: Are there some who are more authentic than others?

A: *I will answer by giving some explanation about Buddhism. In general, in Buddhism it is said, rely not on the person, rely on the doctrine. Similarly, whether the person is valid and reliable or not depends upon what the person is saying. One should not rely just on the fame of the person. Therefore, someone who is going to practice Buddhism must analyze well. If, having analyzed, one finds that it is beneficial and dependable, then it's suitable to engage in that practice. It is said that even if it takes 12 years to engage in such analysis, it's suitable. That's our general attitude.*

I can't say anything about particular people. In general, many people are serving the Buddhist teaching, and that's good. At the same time, it is important to be cautious. In the past, in our own country, and also in China, Mongolia, and Russia, Buddhist monasteries were originally learning centers. This was very good. In some cases, due to social influence, these centers became corrupt. Sometimes it became more like a center for business and money-making than a religious center. So, in the future we must take care. Also, we welcome constructive criticism from our friends. This is very important. Not to just believe too much praising—criticism is very necessary.

Q: There's a strong feeling in the West that for something to be good, it must have some concept of permanence. The religions that had their origin in India do not have this, and I think this is the basic problem that the West has in understanding these other ways of thinking?

A: *The purpose of religion is not for arguing. If we look for differences, we can find many differences. There's no use talking about it. Like Buddha, Jesus Christ, and all other great teachers, they created their own ideas, teachings, with sincere motivation, love, kindness toward humankind, and they shared it for the benefit of humankind. I do not think these great teachers made these differences in order to make more trouble. Because I believe in Buddhism, because I believe there's no creator, if I criticize other religions which believe in a creator, then if Lord Buddha was still here, he might scold me.*

I make distinctions in order to get peace in your own mind, not for criticizing, not for argument or competition. So, Buddhists can't make the whole world population become Buddhist. That's impossible. Christians cannot convert all mankind to Christianity. And Hindus cannot govern all mankind. Over the past many centuries, if you look unbiasedly, each faith, each great teaching, serves mankind very much. So it's much better to make friends and understand each other and make an effort to serve humankind, rather than criticize or argue. This is my belief.

Also, if I say that all religions and philosophies are the same, that is hypocritical, not true. There are differences. I believe there's a 100% possibility to make real peace, and to help, shoulder-to-shoulder, and serve humankind. Equally, we have no responsibility and no right to impose on a non-believer. What's important is, a non-believer or a believer is the same human being; we must have a lot of respect for each other.

Q: Is it possible to have world harmony?

A: *Whether we can achieve world harmony or not, we have no other alternative but to work toward that goal. It is the best alternative we have.*

Q: With the vision of world unity, in your tradition is there any prediction of any such event coming about and is there any record of it existing in the ancient past?

A: *No.*

Q: Individuals almost never say they favor warfare, but they make war. Why?

A: *Basically, it is ignorance. There are many different states of mind. Reasoning is needed when the mind is emotional and thoughts of anger, hatred and attachment are strong. Then it is hopeless to reason. When these feelings are the general atmosphere, then almost always there is tragedy.*

Q: Do you think that some day you will return to a free Tibet?

A: *Certainly.*

Q: How?

A: *That's for time to tell. I can only say that things do change, and already there are communications.*

Q: Do you think the recent political changes within Tibet bode well for the future of your return there?

A: *There are many things changing. A more modern atmosphere is coming, more liberalization. There are some slight changes in Tibet also, but the extent of liberalization that has come in China has not come in Tibet yet.*

Q: What would you like Americans to do about the Chinese presence in Tibet?

A: *We are fighting for our own happiness, our own rights. After all, we Tibetans are human beings. We have the right to live as a human brotherhood, we have the right to gain our happiness. In this country, people always regard the importance of freedom, the importance of liberty, which we also want.*

Q: You have followed the efforts of your wisdom and compassion to regain Tibet. Do you plan to use some other means to get your country back?

A: *Violence, you mean?*

Q: I wasn't asking that. Is there another way that you're planning to get Tibet back?

A: *I always believe, generally speaking, trying to solve problems with true mutual respect, mutual understanding. Definitely we can find it. China has become more moderate recently, but it's too early to say anything definitely. It seems things are changing. That's all.*

Q: Recently, visitors—reporters were allowed into Tibet and talked about the monasteries being open, and so forth. Are people being trained? They said the youngest people they saw conducting services were probably in their 30s and 40s. Is there any training going on in Tibet now of young monks?

A: *No. Since May of this year the Chinese have been publicizing about the uselessness of religion in the Tibetan daily newspaper. On one side they speak of complete freedom of religion and religious practice. At the same time, since May, they've intensified their criticism and reasons about the uselessness of the practice of religion.*

Q: How do you suggest that we, as spiritual people, can effect a spiritual influence, practically speaking, on political affairs?

A: *This is a difficult question. The atmosphere is not healthy. Everyone says peace, but when things are related to self-interest nobody bothers about war, killing, stealing, etc. That's the reality. Under such circumstances, you have to be temperate and practical. We need some long-range policy. I feel deeply that maybe we can find some new type of educational system for the younger generation with an emphasis of love, peace, brotherhood, etc. One or two countries cannot do this, unless it's a world-wide movement. So, practically, we who believe in moral thinking must live our way of life as something truthful, something reasonable, and make it like an example, a demonstration to others, of the value of religion, the value of spirituality. That we can practice, that is our responsibility, before teaching others, before changing others, we ourselves must change. We must be honest, sincere, kindhearted. This is very important. This doesn't just apply to your question. This is the responsibility of all mankind.*

Q: Where does Buddhism stand on social reform?

A: *One of the basic Buddhist philosophies is the theory of interdependence. Many types of good and bad and benefit and harm are determined in Buddhism with respect to the actual situation at the particular time. Therefore, it's difficult with respect to many topics, to say that only one particular way is the correct one. Thus, there have to be many changes.*

Q: Who is the individual responsible to or what are the motives for his moral responsibility?

A: *The reason why we seek to behave in a good manner is that it's from good behavior that good fruits are derived. So, the basic reason is that one wants happiness and doesn't want suffering, and on the basis of that enters into good actions and avoids bad actions. Goodness and badness of actions is determined on the basis of the goodness and badness of the fruits of it. Thus, this involves the Buddhist doctrine of Karma and the effects of action. Similarly in Hinduism, too.*

Q: Is the intention of an action important?

A: *Yes, certainly. Motivation. This is the most important, the keypoint. We make differences between karma, for instance, when one doesn't have the motivation but has done the deed, or has the motivation but hasn't done the deed—and both—and neither.*

Q: There is a breakdown in institutions — in religion and in family. How do you feel that we can reverse that trend?

A: *Through moral ethics, consideration and patience, and more and more tolerance to each other and, of course, compassion. First of all, before people get married, they should decide and be careful, and not go into it in a rushed manner of infatuation. And gradually undertake the right feeling for family life and atmosphere. I feel it is extremely important. When I have seen a child whose parents are divorced, I felt very sorry, because I think the rest of their life somehow it affects them.*

Q: What responsibility do Buddhists have in dealing with people who cause suffering?

A: *You have to make an attempt to stop it.*

Q: Is the difference between the empirical self and the actual self what is common to all religions?

A: *There are differences within the Buddhist schools on this. There are different positions presented with respect to what "I" is. Eight different interpretations! Everyone accepts that there is the mere "I" and that this appears to those whose minds have and have not been affected by systems, and if one denies that there is such an "I" or self, this would contradict direct perception. Because Buddhism asserts selflessness, when one doesn't understand what the word "Self" is or what selflessness means, there's a danger of thinking that there's no "I" or Self at all. If one doesn't accept an "I" or Self, in any way whatsoever, then this would be a falling into an extreme of nihilism.*

Q: You appear to be a very hopeful man. In the past, we've had such great tragedies as the holocaust, tragedies of totalitarian nations, tragedies in this country against Native Americans, yet you're hopeful. What is the basis of your hope?

A: *Hope is the basis of hope. I mean, there is no guarantee, but it's better to hope, and try. Actually, our basic human way of life is on the basis of hope. In the long hope is that the truth will overcome. Historically, we've had all those bad fights, but it never remains forever, sooner or later that will cease, that will diminish.*

Greeting the Dalai Lama for the government of Ontario the Honourable Reuben Baetz, minister of culture, said, "Your Holiness' visit to Canada is not only a memorable occasion for us, but it is also a spiritual event for Canada, because this is the first time that His Holiness or a Dalai Lama of Tibet has set foot in Canada. We are overjoyed to have our wish fulfilled by your Holiness' acceptance of our invitation to visit us."

Tibetan-Canadian childen, holding the Tibetan flag, greet His Holiness on his arrival in Toronto.

First I would like to express my kindness to the government and people of Canada, because this country has more than 400 Tibetan refugees settled here in their new, second home—at least I hope temporarily. So they are very happy. They often come to India on pilgrimage, and especially to pursue their own religion. And I am glad to be able to express that they are very happy in this country. So I must take this opportunity to express thanks.

Actually, the first time I was in the United States, I thought I would be able to visit Canada too. But then, due to time, I postponed it.

As you know, my visit here is not political; it is mainly religion and culture. So now I am looking forward to visiting a new country for about two weeks, and also to visiting some individual organizations who are helping the Tibetan project, creating various Tibetan centers, and also education opportunities for the younger Tibetans, and also some rehabilitation projects. I take this opportunity to thank those organizations.

His Holiness arriving at the Royal York Hotel in Toronto.

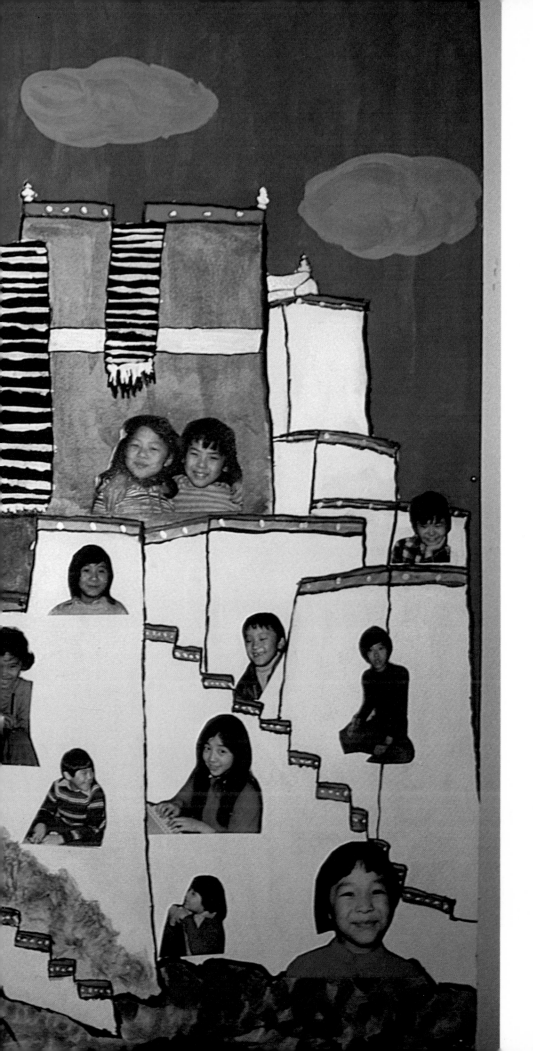

Painting done by Tibetan children in Montreal.

Today, human society's major problem is human rights. Through highly developed scientific technology, we can solve any material human problem such as poverty, disease, etc., but at the same time, due to this same technology, we create more fear and more desire. For example, today we fear a sudden explosion of atoms in the world. That sort of thing has become a reality.

Now you see, if we have such fears, of potential destruction from the atom bomb, we will suffer greatly from them unless we have inner peace. On top of the usual human suffering, we have more fear, more constant threat. So therefore we need more the teachings of kindness and feelings of brotherhood.

In order to live together on this planet, we need kindness, we need a kind atmosphere, rather than an angry atmosphere. To solve problems, we need a warm atmosphere.

So, although there are various social religious factors that may differ, all religions have this goal of creating inner peace.

Tibetan women fold the traditional white ceremonial scarves (khatas) for presentation to His Holiness.

Tibetan-Canadian childen waiting for His Holiness' arrival in Montreal.

We need to clearly recognize that the basic aim of all religions is the same. Since all religions are for the sake of taming one's own mind, to make one a better person, we need to bring all religious practice into a healing of our own mind. It's not at all good, and extremely unfortunate, to use the doctrines and practices that are for the sake of taming the mind as a reason for becoming biased. Therefore it is extremely important for us to be non-sectarian. As Buddhists we need to respect the Christians, the Jews, the Hindus and so on. And also among Buddhists we shouldn't make distinctions that some are Theravadin and some are of the Great Vehicle and so forth; we are all the same in having the same teacher. If we become more sundered under this influence of bias due to obscuration, then there is no end to it. Therefore, we need to recognize that the religious doctrines are for the sake of taming the mind, and use them that way.

Audience at Interfaith Service, at Queen Mary Cathedral in Montreal.

His Holiness the Dalai Lama in the Queen Mary Cathedral, in Montreal.

In order to increase the sense of cherishing others, it is first important to think about the faults of cherishing one's self and the good qualities of cherishing others. If we cherish others, both others and ourselves, both deeply and superficially, will be happy. Whether in terms of the family, or the family of nations as a whole world, if we take the cherishing of others as the very basis of policy for our format, then we will be able to succeed in our common effort. Most of the good or beneficial effects that come about in the world, come based on an attitude of cherishing others.

The opposite is also true: When we cherish ourselves more than others, both superficially and deeply we produce various types of suffering, both for ourselves and for those around us. Therefore we need to make effort at the root of this goodness, that is to say, this good heart, warm heart.

Now we have to consider, if we want to increase the basic good attitude, that the type of closeness that we have for the class of our own friends is very small and it cannot be extended forever. What we have to do, however, is to change it and increase it and extend it. Now it is the case that, whoever it is, whether it is oneself or any other, no matter who it is, each of us wants happiness and doesn't want suffering. We are equal in this way. And both oneself and others have the right to get rid of suffering and to gain happiness. On this basis of these equalities, oneself is only one, whereas others are infinite in number.

The many scriptures set forth in the teachings of Buddha are included in three scriptural collections. How is it that all of the Buddha's teachings are included in three scriptural collections? It is that the Buddha set forth the three trainings. The three trainings are included in the three scriptural collections, because each of them serves as the means of expressing mainly one of those collections, one of those trainings. What are the three trainings? They are the trainings in ethics—the trainings as set forth include the mode of behavior. Then there is the training in meditative stabilization, which explains how to meditate. The Dharma is practiced indeed by way of body, speech and mind, but it is mainly by way of mind. One needs to tame the mind. One needs a strong mind, a concentrated mind; therefore one needs to develop calm abiding. In the effort to attain wisdom, what we don't want is suffering, and in order to get rid of suffering, we need the intelligence that can discriminate between the good and bad and so forth; therefore we need wisdom.

The scriptures that take these three respectively as the main object of teaching are the scriptural collection of discipline, the scriptural collection of the set of discourses, and the scriptural collection of knowledge. The training in ethics is concerned with behavior; the training in meditative stabilization is concerned with meditation; the training in wisdom is concerned with view. There is the triad; view, behavior, and meditation. The scriptures set forth a mode by which one's view, behavior and meditation will not fall in either of the two extremes.

The scriptures on discipline sets forth modes of behavior for a lay person and for monks and nuns. In the discipline, it sets forth a prohibition of the extremes of having too good clothing, food, shelter, and so forth. And the Buddha also prohibited the extreme of self-torture, in which one engages in too much fasting, or wears clothing that is not appropriate such that it brings suffering to one's self. Therefore, our proper behavior is achieved in the proper context of not falling into either of these two extremes. As Shantideva said in his Engaging in Bodhisattva Deeds, *"The main thing is to consider the situation; what is needed in the situation."*

When one puts these precepts into practice, one needs to consider that which is to be done, and the purpose. For instance, for a monk or a nun, it is not permitted to eat after 2 p.m. However, there are exceptions. For instance, if a person has an illness such that if that person didn't eat, it would increase the illness. Similarly, also one is not allowed to lie. For instance, if someone would have a vow to tell the truth, and is in the woods, and sees an animal run off in a certain direction, and then the hunter comes along and asks the person where the animal went, there is a prohibition against lying, but the purpose here would be for the sake of saving the life of that animal. Therefore, at that time, the person who even had the vow not to lie can say, "Oh, I really didn't see anything," or "I saw something in the trees." Illustrated by this, one has to take into account that which is prohibited and the probable benefit of doing something some other way, and do that which is more beneficial.

Then, with respect to meditation: For instance, if one's mind comes under the influence of factors that are not consistent with meditative stabilization, such as excitement or laxity, then that is one extreme. The purpose of overcoming the distractions of laxity or excitement is to make one's mind so that one is capable of meditating on the actual mode of existence of phenomena, so that one can cultivate a true view, but if one, having gotten rid of laxity and excitement, only cultivates a non-conceptual state, then that is an extreme, and that non-conceptual state will only lead to another lifetime of rebirth in cyclical existence, in a higher type of realm.

So roughly speaking, that is a way of avoiding the two extremes, through the effects of meditation.

Then when one explains the view, this is done in terms of the two truths. Sometimes this is expressed as appearance and emptiness. All systems, whether Buddhist or non-Buddhist, present their view in terms of avoiding the *two extremes of permanence and nihilism: The Santyas, the Vedantas, or within Buddhism, the Vaibhasikas, the Sautrantikas, the Chittamatrins and the Madhyamikas.*

For instance, within the Buddhist systems themselves, from within their own specific viewpoint, each of them, to their own mind, has set forth a view that avoids the two extremes. However, when their views are analyzed with subtle reasoning, then the higher school finds the lower schools to have fallen into extremes of permanence or nihilism. So then, how is it that the higher schools can refute the lower, given that both are based on Buddhist teachings?

In the Buddhist system, the Buddha set forth the four reliances: Do not rely on the person; rely on the doctrine. You cannot say that a doctrine is to be valued just because a person who teaches it is something wonderful. Rather, it is the case that whether the person is reliable or not is to be proved in dependence upon the reliability or lack of reliability of the doctrine that the person teaches.

Then, with respect to the doctrine, one shouldn't rely on the euphony, and so forth, of the word, but look to the profundity of those words. Then, with respect to the teachings, one should not rely on the meaning to be interpreted, but on the definitive meaning. And with respect to the meaning, one should not rely on the consciousness that is deluded or affected by dualistic perception, but should rely on an exalted wisdom consciousness, free from such dualistic appearances.

Therefore, the teacher, Buddha himself, said, "Oh monks and nuns, you should not accept my teaching just out of respect for me, but should analyze it, the way that a goldsmith analyzes gold by rubbing, cutting and melting.'' Therefore, although Buddha himself set forth several means of distinguishing his own scriptures with respect to whether they were definitive or interpretable, it is by reasoning that we must determine which is definitive and which is interpretable.

Thus it is that the entire system, with subtler and subtler reasoning, shows that the two of the lower systems fall into the two extremes. How is it, in the Madhyamika system, that they avoid the two extremes? They avoid the extreme of permanence by viewing that phenomena do not exist in their own right. And it is through that knowledge of how to present all the actions, objects of cyclic existence and nirvana—how to present all phenomena within the context of their not inherently existing, but existing conventionally, validly, that they avoid the extreme of non-existence or nihilism.

It is truly mind that sees the actual mode of subsistence of phenomena. It is the mind that acts as an antidote to the types of aimless consciousness that misconceive the nature of phenomena. And it is through removing that ignorance that one can remove the desire and hatred and so forth that are induced by that ignorance. When one can stop that, one can stop the accumulation of contaminated action, or karma. Through stopping that, one stops birth. Through stopping birth, one stops suffering. Such a training in wisdom can only be achieved by the mind, therefore it is necessary to make the mind serviceable. Therefore, I see it as necessary prior to the training in wisdom to engage in the training of meditative stabilization.

The Dalai Lama speaking at the Vancouver Institute, in British Columbia.

Audience listening to the Dalai Lama at Vancouver Institute.

If you have love and compassion toward all sentient beings, particularly towards your enemy, that is the true love and compassion. Now the kind of love or compassion that you have toward your friends, your wife and children, is essentially not true kindness. That is attachment. That kind of love cannot be infinite.

It is not being said that in order to generate a consciousness arisen through hearing or arisen from thinking that realizes emptiness, it is necessary at first to engage in training of meditative stabilization. What is being said is that in order to generate a consciousness which has arisen from meditation, and realizes emptiness, it is necessary at first to engage in the training of meditative stabilization.

In order to overcome the internal distractions within the mind, it is necessary at first to overcome the distractions of body and speech through proper ethics. Therefore, the training in ethics is set forth first. But the series of degree is set forth in their series of practices. That is the explanation of how to avoid the two extremes in relation to the three trainings.

You new Buddhists in Western society need also to avoid the two extremes. One of these extremes would be complete isolation from the general way of life, and also from society. That is the same thing. It is better to remain in society and to lead a general way of life. That's my belief.

And the other extreme would be to become completely absorbed in this worldly life, to become so involved in making money that one becomes a part in a machine. So you have to avoid those two extremes.

You have to practice kindness and follow the teachings. At the same time, if you always practice tolerance, compassion, sometimes, some people may take advantage of you. On that occasion, without losing your internal calmness, your internal compassion, you may take action of some nature in order to prevent someone from taking advantage of you. That is a practical way. You have to avoid the extreme, too, of being taken advantage of. At all times, one needs to avoid the two extremes. If you get too hungry, the same—if you gorge yourself, the same also.

So my true religion is kindness. If you practice kindness as you live, no matter if you are learned or not learned, whether you believe in the next life or not, whether you believe in God or Buddha or some other religion, in day-to-day life, you have to be a kind person. With this motivation, whether you are a practitioner or a lawyer or politician or administrator, worker, engineer, no matter. Whatever your profession or field, you carry your work as a professional. In the meantime, deep down, you are a kind person. This is something useful in our daily life.

At right, His Holiness gives the Lam Rim teachings in Canada. Below, his personal attendants, Thupten Ngawang (left) and Losang Gawa (right), who travelled with him from Dharamsala, India to Canada.

To increase your compassion, visualize yourself, first, as a neutral person. Then on the right side, visualize your old self as a person who is only seeking for his or her own welfare, who doesn't think at all about other people, who would take advantage of anyone at any time whenever the chance arises, and who is never content. Visualize your old self that way on the right.

Then on the other side of your neutral self, visualize a group of persons who are really suffering and need some help. Now think: all humans have the natural desire to be happy and to avoid suffering; all humans equally have the right to be happy and to get rid of suffering. Now you think—wisely, not selfishly —and even if some selfishness must be there, think in a widely selfish way, not in a narrowminded selfish way: Everybody wants happiness; nobody wants foolishness or wants that type of selfish, discontent person.

So you see, if we want to be a good person, a more reasonable, logical person, then we don't want to be like this narrow-minded selfish person on the right. You don't want to join this single, selfish, greedy, discontent person on the right. It's almost like making a line between the single selfish person and the group: You would want to join that group.

When we practice this technique of visualization, naturally the majority side wins our heart. As much as you come closer to the majority side, so much do you become farther away from this selfishness. Because the mediator of this is yourself, your own sense of altruism will increase and increase. If you practice this way daily, it will be helpful.

Two Tibetan-Canadian sisters awaiting His Holiness.

◄ *His Holiness the Dalai Lama with Gyalwa Karmapa in Toronto.*

His Holiness and Jean Darpeau, the Mayor of Montreal, at the Montreal City Hall.

Tibetans in Calgary waiting for His Holiness' arrival.

If we use this human brain for something that is of little import, it would be very sad. If we spend our time, just concerned with the affairs of this lifetime, up to the point of death, it is very sad and very weak. We need to decide that it is completely perverse. When you think in this manner, the emphasis just on this lifetime becomes weaker and weaker. It is said that we should renounce this life. It doesn't mean that we should go hungry or not take care of this lifetime at all, but that we should reduce our attachment to affairs that are limited to this lifetime. Now when we reduce the emphasis on the appearances of this lifetime, and the appearances of future lifetimes come to the mind, it is necessary to investigate those also. Because in the future, even though one attains a good lifetime, there will be a lifetime after that lifetime, and a lifetime after that lifetime.

These four Native American chieftains drove from upstate New York to Canada to have an audience with His Holiness and to perform a fire ceremony with him. Left to right, Thomas Banyacya, a Hopi elder, Leon Shenandoah, Chief of the Six Nations, Vince Johnson, an Onondaga chief, and Oren Lyons, an Onondaga chief.

◄ *His Holiness the Dalai Lama with American Indian chiefs having a fire ceremony at the Royal York Hotel in Toronto.*

His Holiness speaking to a group of Canadians in Calgary.

If you tame your mind, happiness comes. If you don't tame your mind, there is no way to be happy. It is necessary to fix up the mind. It is through the appearance of these afflicted emotions in our mind that we are drawn into various bad actions and so forth. But if these afflicted emotions which appear in the expanse of the nature of the mind can be extinguished back into the nature of the mind, then the afflicted emotions and actions and so forth that are built on them will stop. As Milarepa said, "Like clouds appearing from space and disappearing back into space."

If our mind is dominated by anger, we will lose the best part of the human brain: wisdom, the ability to decide between what is right and what is wrong. Anger is the most serious problem facing the world today.

All major religions are basically the same in that they emphasize peace of mind and kindness; but it is very important to practice this in our daily lives, not just in a church or a temple.

I hope that you who are graduating from St. Thomas University today will combine religious and moral teachings with your education. You are now starting to lead the real life, which is not an easy thing in modern society, whether it is the east or the west. The future may not be easy, but I hope you will always be able to use wisdom and intelligence in deciding what is right and what is wrong.

Graduation procession at St. Thomas University, Fredericton, Canada.

The Dalai Lama receiving an honorary degree at St. Thomas University, Fredericton, Canada.

I am very much honored by receiving this degree from you, and I am particularly honored that I have gotten a degree without having to do much studying.

Now I am going to say something about the purpose of religion.

Human beings are of such nature that they should have not only material facilities but spiritual requirements as well. Without spiritual requirements, it is difficult to get and maintain peace of mind.

To maintain wisdom, it is necessary to have inner strength. Without inner development, sometimes we may not retain selfconfidence and courage. If we lose these things life will be difficult. The impossible can be possible with will power.

There is no sense in just being attached to this lifetime, because no matter how long you live, in this type of life, which nowadays at the longest is around 100 years, at that time you must die. At least then; otherwise it's not definite when one will die, and no matter how much wealth and resources you have in this lifetime, it won't help at all at that point.

If we become very rich, even becoming millionaires or billionaires, on the day of our death, no matter how much money we have in the bank, there isn't any little piece of it that we can take with us. The death of a rich person and the death of a wild animal is just the same.

The mind of enlightenment is the wish for clear enlightenment, complete and perfect enlightenment, for the sake of others. In cultivating in detail this altruistic mind of enlightenment, that has these two intentions of helping others and achieving one's own enlightenment in order to do that, there are two streams of transmission of instruction, the one being from Asanga, which is the Sevenfold Cause and Effect Instructions, *and the other being the* Switching of Self and Other, *transmitted through Nagarjuna to Shantideva, Shantideva being the one who explained it in great detail.*

Shantideva's Engaging in Bodhisattva Deeds *is really excellent for this. Nagarjuna also sets forth a brief and fundamental way in his* Precious Garland. *Use* Precious Garland *as the root text, and use Shantideva as the explanation of it. For those who want to generate this altruistic mind of enlightenment, these two are really necessary.*

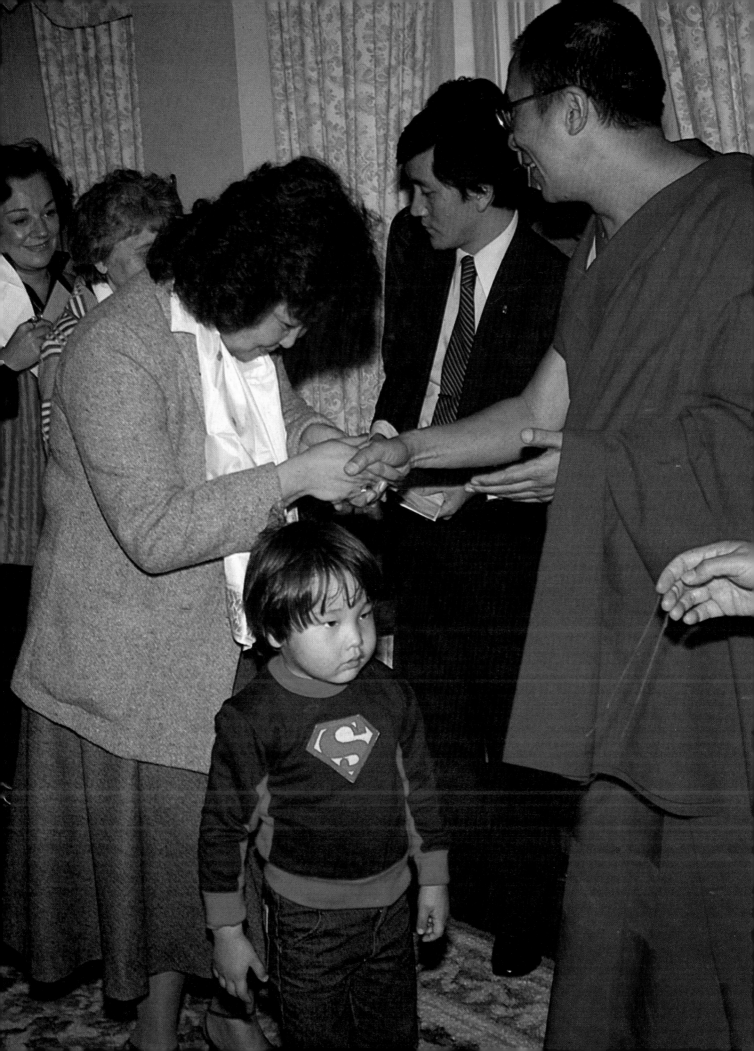

His Holiness the Dalai Lama visiting a Tibetan temple in Longueuil, Canada.

Geshe Kyenrab Tobgyal, founder of the Tibetan Temple in Longueuil, standing in front of the al

◄ *His Holiness the Dalai Lama with his senior tutor, Kyabje Ling Rinpoche.*

One should cultivate, in meditation, an attitude of equanimity, and then meditate on all sentient beings as being mothers, fathers, brothers and sisters. Once one generates this attitude of equanimity for the three beings, having gotten over the desire and hatred, one needs to remove the factor of neglect that can be present when people are viewed equally. This can be done in two different ways: one, through generating a sense of altruism, wishing to help those beings because they want happiness and don't want suffering, and the other is to reflect upon the kindness of those beings towards oneself. It is through reflecting on how sentient beings have helped oneself, have been one's father and mother and so forth, over the continuum of lifetimes, and that it would be unsuitable to deny them proper help, that one can train the attitude of wishing for help and happiness for sentient beings.

When one gets used to these types of thoughts, the mind can be gradually trained. Someone who is extremely selfish, who begins to cultivate such habits, will gradually become less and less selfish. So then this is how one generates the sense of altruism for others.

The Dalai Lama with Trappist monks, in Montreal.

If, in all situations, no matter what the mind is doing, from a corner of the mind, one is still intensely seeking the welfare of sentient beings, and seeking enlightenment for the sake of them, then one has generated a fully qualified altruistic mind of enlightenment. These types of realizations are not such that when you generate them, the whole world turns around for them. One's disposition changes gradually, gradually.

If you cultivate this slowly, steadily, over a period of time, then when five, ten years have passed, when you consider your way of life, your way of thinking and so forth, how it was before and how it is now, then you can see the difference.

Liberation cannot be sought from the outside through something else; like someone else giving it to you. When one has achieved liberation, due to the fact that one has removed all afflicted emotions, then, no matter what kind of external conditions one meets with, one will not generate any of the afflicted emotions. Thus one will not newly accumulate any new karma. The cycle has been stopped.

Therefore, the attainment or the non-attainment of liberation depends on the removal or the non-removal of the afflicted emotions, the chief of which is ignorance. The process of liberation depends on the removal of the afflicted emotions, and that depends on wisdom, and wisdom depends on the thought definitely to get out of cyclic existence. Initially it is very important to develop the intention to leave cyclic existence.

Interfaith service at Christ Church in Vancouver, Canada.

His Holiness the Dalai Lama giving blessings in Vancouver.

The reason the Buddha made this display of leaving all the facilities of a household and becoming a monk, going into retreat, meditating and so forth, was in order to indicate to us, his followers, what we should do. If the Buddha had to work very hard to achieve realization, it's pretty much impossible that we could achieve the same realization by taking it easy.

If you get to the point where a corner of your mind is continuously involved with this wish to achieve highest enlightenment for the sake of sentient beings, then that's the time when this altruistic mind of enlightenment needs to be conjoined with the actual rite of mind generation— the wishing rite of generating the mind of enlightenment.

And having done that, one needs to train in the causes that prevent that aspiration of mind from deteriorating in this lifetime or in later lifetimes. It is not sufficient just to generate this aspiration. One needs to generate the actual mind of enlightenment, the actual intention to become enlightened for the sake of others. The intention alone is not sufficient; one needs to train in order to understand that it is necessary to engage in the practices to bring about full enlightenment; these being the practices of the six perfections (giving, ethics, patience, effort, concentration and wisdom), or the 10 perfections.

Now having trained in the wish to generate the actual mind of enlightenment, it is necessary to undertake the Bodhisattva vows. If, having taken the Bodhisattva vows, one's practice of the Bodhisattva deeds is going well, then it is possible to enter into the practice of Tantra or Mantra.

His Holiness teaching in Calgary, Canada.

In order to generate the thought to get out of cyclic existence, it is necessary to know about the good qualities of liberation, and the faults of cyclic existence that one wants to get out of. However, what is cyclic existence? As Dharma-kirti says, it can be posited as the burden of mental and physical aggregates which are assumed out of contaminated action. Therefore, cyclic existence doesn't refer to some sort of country or area. When you look into it, cyclical existence can be identified as the burden of these mental and physical aggregates which we have assumed from our own contaminated actions and afflicted emotions.

When once we have such contaminated aggregates, they serve as a basis of suffering in the present. Because they are under the influence of former contaminated actions and afflicted emotions, they are devoid of being under their own power.

That they are not under their own power indicates that even though one wants happiness and doesn't want suffering, since we have this type of mind and body which is under the influence of former contaminated actions and afflictions, we are beset by many sufferings. And these contaminated mental and physical aggregates also induce suffering in the future.

It is one thing to explain the Dharma from the mouth, but it is very hard to put it into practice. If you don't put the Dharma into practice, however, there is no way for a good fruit to become ripe just from explaining. If the cause is just something explained from the mouth, the effect would be just something explained from the mouth, and that wouldn't help much, would it? When we are hungry, what we need is some actual food. It's not going to help for someone to say, "Oh, French food is very tasty, English food is very tasty," and so forth. In time you will get fed up with the person just saying these things to you, and will be in danger of getting angry. When I indicate the path of liberation to you, you need to put it into practice. Shantideva says, "As it is with medicine, it's not sufficient just to touch it, it is necessary to take the medicine internally."

His Holiness the Dalai Lama blessing monks at the Tibetan temple in Toronto.

An altar with water bowls and butter sculpture at the Tibetan Buddhist temple in Toronto.

His Holiness the Dalai Lama giving a sermon at the Tibetan Buddhist temple in Toronto. ▶

The questions and answers presented below were compiled from the Dalai Lama's numerous public and private lectures, scholarly seminars, private meetings, and news conferences throughout his visit to Canada. As in the first part of this book, they represent those varied issues he addressed during his Canadian tour.

Q: Your Holiness, has your exile from Tibet brought about changes in Tibetan philosophy?

A: *Philosophy? I don't think so. The Buddhist philosophy is based on reason. Philosophy is the main point of my country. The essence of Dharma will not change. As far as reality remains the same, philosophy will be the same. As long as humans face suffering, there will remain the Dharma, which deals not only with human beings, but with all sentient beings in this condition.*

Q: From a national level, does altruism run the risk of sacrifice? How do you practice altruism for a neighbor who seeks to destroy you?

A: *That is a complicated question. From this viewpoint, our second generation, the refugees, is more the problem. You see, it would be better to forget than to continue to hold anger, but it is very complicated because in the future we don't know where we will be. So there is no other alternative but to think we have to do something for the growth of kindness. We have to think and work to make a new world.*

Actually, in our life there is no telling if you will live tomorrow, but we are doing our usual business in the hope that we will survive tomorrow. Though there is no telling what the future will hold, one must do something, and try to do something. This is the right thing.

Q: Your Holiness, can you explain how your successor might be chosen, due to the changes in the situation in Tibet, as to the way in which you were chosen, as you explained. And can you explain how any changes might be made in the way of succession?

A: *I have not much worry about it. If the Tibetan people feel it necessary to choose another small Dalai Lama, all right, then they will choose a Dalai Lama. If people feel it not necessary, not much better to do so, then no Dalai Lama will exist. But that's not my responsibility. I hope I'll remain for some time. But choosing another Dalai Lama is the next generation's responsibility.*

Q: You had spoken about the notions of kindness and selfishness, suffering and happiness mainly from the point of view of the single person. But how do groups such as nations achieve kindness, unselfishness and happiness? What is the step from the individual to the group? How can one make a group altruistic?

A: *Groups are composed of individual persons. Our atmosphere and environment nowadays is very strained, not a very peaceful one. In our atmosphere today, things are decided by money and power. This is not right. The present atmosphere is due to our own mode of thinking. Now in order to change it, first, we have to, as individuals, take the initiative in trying to develop certain good human qualities. First of all, we need to make a demonstration of what a good attitude and a good mode of behavior is, person by person by single person, then gradually, over time, build groups that have this attitude. Now, with this education, how do we utilize this education? If a person really has altruism, then as much as that person gains knowledge of various sufferings, so much can that person put it to use to help others.*

Q: Your Holiness, would you give us a brief outline of how you came to your spiritual mission in your life?

A: *It seems I feel my mission is, wherever I am, to express my feeling about the importance of kindness and the true sense of brotherhood. This I always feel, and I myself practice this. For the Tibetan community I express these things, and I advise them on the importance of kindness and on the need to develop less attachment, more tolerance, more contentment. These are very useful and very important. Generally, wherever I go, in the United States, in Europe, in Mongolia, I stress the importance of kindness, and it seems to me that generally people agree with my feelings. So I feel that they hold my vision also.*

Anyway, from my side, I am trying to uplift real human brotherhood. I think human harmony is based on a true sense of brotherhood. As a Buddhist, it doesn't matter whether we are believers or non-believers, educated or uneducated, easterner or westerner or northerner or southerner, so long as we are the same human beings with the same kind of flesh and the same kind of features. Everyone wants happiness and doesn't want sorrow, and we have every right to be happy.

Sometimes we humans put too much importance on secondary matters, such as differences of political system or economic system or race. There seem to be many discriminations due to these differences. But comparatively basic human well-being is not based on these things. So I always try to understand the real human values. All these different philosophies or religious systems are supposed to serve human happiness. But here is something wrong, when there is too much emphasis on these secondary matters, these differences in systems which are supposed to serve human happiness. When human values are lost for these things, it is not much good.

So, in a few words, it seems my mission is the propagation of true kindness, genuine kindness and compassion. I myself practice these things. And it gives me more happiness, more success. If I practice anger, or jealousy, or bitterness, then I am sure I will give the wrong impression. More sadness. No doubt my smile would disappear if I practice more anger. If I practice more sincerity or kindness, it gives me more pleasure. Despite as an unfortunate person.

Q: Your Holiness, if you were to go back to Tibet, would it be as a political and religious figure, or would it be only as a spiritual leader?

A: *At the time, there is no question of returning. Now, in fact, that is a political question. At the moment, things are not at all good. Also, comparatively some things are improving. The leaders in Peking clearly realize that the conditions in Tibet are very poor, very bad. So they openly admitted their past policy regarding Tibet is a complete failure. They are trying to find a new way of approach to the problem. I quite admire their courage in admitting their past policy. So I am hoping that there will be improvements.*

There is still suffering in Tibet. If the majority of our people genuinely decide that they are happy, then of course I will decide the old question of whether to return or not. At the moment it is not possible. You see, my very purpose of coming out of Tibet was for our own country. I spent nine years with the Chinese. After 1959, I became a refugee. If we could not serve our people from within our own country, it has been our experience that being outside has been much more helpful for our own people. So you see, until the inside situation becomes truly, genuinely satisfactory, I will not return. I believe I can better serve our people, the six millon people of Tibet, from outside.

Q: Your Holiness, would you give a few more words about the nature of the journey to inner peace?

A: *It is helpful to distinguish the five paths—the paths of accumulation, of preparation, of seeing, of meditation, and of no more worrying. The path of accumulation generates the output, the mind of enlightenment. Then one practices the six perfections. In the six perfections one develops right practice of the perfection of concentration and wisdom. And when, through developing the perfection of concentration and wisdom, one develops a state arisen from meditation in which one realizes emptiness, then one has attained the path of preparation. When one gets used to that realization, and all dualistic experience is removed and there is no pollution by dualistic appearance, then one realizes the infinite correctly and one arrives at the path of seeing. At that time one attains the first stage or ground. Then one needs to attain the path of meditation, which is a matter of getting used to the emptiness which one has already realized correctly. At the time of the path of seeing, one is able to remove the conception of inherent existence, which is promoted by artificial thinking and so on. Then one needs to progress over the second, third and fourth grounds up to the tenth ground. At the beginning of the eighth ground, one gets rid of the obstruction of the innate conception of inherent existence as well as its seeds. Then over the rest of the eighth, ninth, and tenth grounds, one gets rid of the coarser and subtler levels of the obstruction to omniscience. The last moment of the tenth ground is called the vajra of right meditative stabilization. In its second period, one attains omniscience. This the explanation to it.*

Q: Do you believe that there is a view of religion that will unify mankind internationally?

A: *I think it's helpful to have many different religions, since our human mind always likes different approaches for different dispositions. Just like food. There are some people who prefer bread and some who prefer rice, and some who prefer flour. Each has different tastes, and each eats food that accords with his own taste. Some eat rice, some eat flour, but there is no quarrel. Nobody says, ''Oh, you are eating rice.'' In the same way, there is mental variety; so for certain people the Christian religion is more useful, more applicable. It's a basic belief. Some people say, ''There's a god, there's a creator, and everything depends on his acts, so you should be impressed because of the creator.'' You see, if that sort of thing gives you more security, more belief, you will prefer that approach. For such people, that philosophy is the best. Also certain people say our Buddhist belief, that there is no creator and that everything depends on you, you should be impressed—that that is preferable. You see, if you are master, then everything depends on you. For certain people, that way of seeing is much more preferable, much more suitable.*

So from that point of view it is better to have variety, to have many religions.

Now if these words are helpful for you, then put them into practice. But if they aren't helpful, then there's no need for them.

By His Holiness, Tenzin Gyatso,
The Fourteenth Dalai Lama

My Land and My People
McGraw-Hill, New York; Weidenfeld & Nicolson, London, 1962. Panther Books, London, 1964. Potala Publications, Potala Corporation, New York, 1978.

The Opening of the Wisdom Eye
Quest Books, Theosophical Publishing House, Wheaton, Illinois, Madras and London, 1975.

The Buddhism of Tibet and the Key to the Middle Way
The Wisdom of Tibet Series, George Allen & Unwin, London, 1975. Harper and Row, New York, Evanston, San Francisco, London, 1975.

Tantra in Tibet
The Great Exposition of Secret Mantra, by Tsong-ka-pa, Introduced by His Holiness the Dalai Lama, translated by Jeffrey Hopkins, The Wisdom of Tibet Series, George Allen & Unwin, London, Boston, Sydney, 1977.